# CITIES IN CRISIS

Tony Reynolds

Rourke Enterprises, Inc.
Vero Beach, FL 32964

# World Issues

The Arms Trade
Cities in Crisis
Endangered Wildlife
The Energy Crisis
The Environment
The Exploitation of Space
Food or Famine?
Human Rights
The International Debt Crisis

The International Drug Trade
International Terrorism
Nuclear Power
Nuclear Weapons
Population Growth
Refugees
Sports and Politics
Threatened Cultures
World Health

**Cover:** A shanty in New Delhi, India. The housing shortage is a problem that affects cities in both the developing and the developed world.
**Frontispiece:** A traffic jam in central London. Some cities are now so congested that traffic moves more slowly than it did a hundred years ago.

Text © 1990 Rourke Enterprises, Inc.

**Library of Congress Cataloging-in-Publication Data**
Reynolds, Tony, 1936–
    Cities in crisis.

(World issues).
    Includes bibliographical references.
    Summary: Discusses the nature and growth of cities, how they are kept alive or polluted, who controls them, and their possible future.
    1. Cities and towns – Juvenile literature. 2. Urbanization – Juvenile literature. [1. Cities and towns. 2. Urbanization] I. Title. II. Series: World issues (Vero Beach, Fla.).
HT151.R45   1989   307.76   89–10971
ISBN 0–86592–118–0

# Contents

# 1
# The growth of cities

Imagine yourself in a satellite in outer space, looking back down on the Earth. The world's cities would be the most obvious and widespread evidence of human life. Even from high above the Earth's surface, you would be able to make out the cities, with their masses of buildings, roads and railroads, scattered across the globe.

During the past hundred years, the number and size of the world's cities have grown rapidly. By 1950, about 15 percent of the world's population lived in cities with more than 100,000 inhabitants. By 1990, this proportion had doubled to around 30 percent; and by the year 2000, at least four in ten human beings will spend their lives as city dwellers.

Cities can be pleasant and exciting places to live; they are usually important centers of political and cultural activity, where many different kinds of people have the opportunity to meet, live and work together. Yet, increasingly, many cities also seem to be the focus of trouble and conflicts. Urban problems from around the world are brought home to us every day by television and radio reports. Everyone can see pictures of homeless people sleeping on the streets of New York; slums in Calcutta; air pollution in Tokyo; violence and bombings in Belfast; and traffic congestion in Los Angeles. Sometimes the action of human beings can seem to be at its worst in the world's cities.

Why do our cities experience so many different problems? Is there a crisis of confidence in city life? What could be done to make the world's cities better and happier places in which to live?

## What is a city?

Cities existed as long as 5,000 years ago. Often they first developed as the centers of large empires or tribal areas. In various parts of the world, farmers began to produce food surpluses, which supported other members of the community who gathered together in the first towns and cities. Artisans, merchants,

*Homelessness is a major problem in many of the world's cities. The man in this photograph is sleeping on the steps of a New York museum.*

religious leaders, warriors and monarchs were all sustained in their cities by the products of the countryside.

Gradually, cities grew and developed. Babylon in Iraq, Ch'ang-an in China, Mohenjo-Daro in Pakistan, Athens in Greece and Rome in Italy were all important cities in the ancient world. They had large populations and complicated social structures. Archeologists and historians have shown that, even in the past, city life had its problems too. Ancient Rome declined

*The city of Machu Picchu, high in the Andes mountains of Peru in South America. During the eighth century, these deserted ruins were a thriving city.*

rapidly during the fourth century because of internal political conflict and invasions. In China, Ch'ang-an had a population of a million people in 750, but within a hundred years, political problems and rebellions had left most of the city derelict.

7

Although wealthy and important cities have existed throughout history, until fairly recently city life has been the exception rather than the rule. Before the nineteenth century, the vast majority of people still lived in the countryside; and the process of urbanization, the development of towns and cities, has only really been underway over the last two hundred years.

The first country to experience large-scale urbanization was Britain during the Industrial Revolution of the early nineteenth century. There, new towns and cities grew as modern industry developed. People moved away from rural areas to work in the new factories; and even though conditions in the towns were often squalid and unhealthy, the death rate fell, and in general, people began to live longer.

British society changed dramatically in the nineteenth century. In 1801, only one tenth of the population lived in cities of more than 100,000 inhabitants. By 1840, one fifth of the population lived in cities, and by 1900, one third were city dwellers. The same process of urbanization and industrialization soon took place in other countries of the world, such as Germany and Japan. In the United States, there was rapid urbanization over the sixty years from 1880 to 1940.

Today, urbanization is still taking place, and many countries in the developing world, such as Mexico, Brazil and India, are experiencing urbanization faster than ever before. However, in these countries urbanization is not always accompanied by an equal growth in industry. The development of cities today is often stimulated more by overpopulation in the surrounding countryside than by industrialization in the city itself. Moreover, the cities of the developing world are larger than ever before; Cairo, Manila and Buenos Aires are all now twice as big as London, which for many years was the biggest city in the world.

*These three maps show the world's ten biggest cities in 1900, 1950 and the year 2000. In 1900, London was the largest city, with 6.4 million people. In 2000, the world's biggest city will be Mexico City, with 31 million inhabitants.*

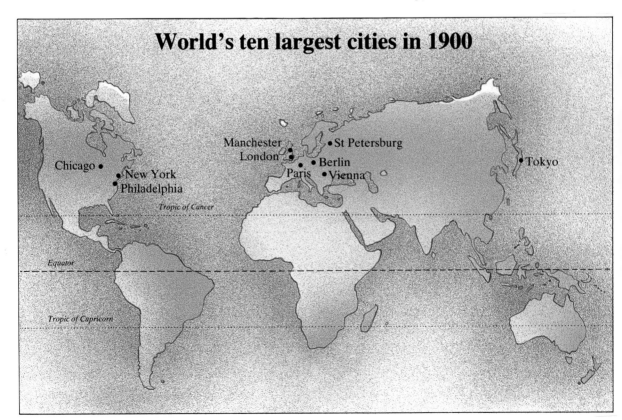

**World's ten largest cities in 1900**

Chicago • 
• New York
• Philadelphia
*Tropic of Cancer*
Manchester •
London •
Paris • • Berlin
• Vienna
• St Petersburg
• Tokyo
*Equator*
*Tropic of Capricorn*

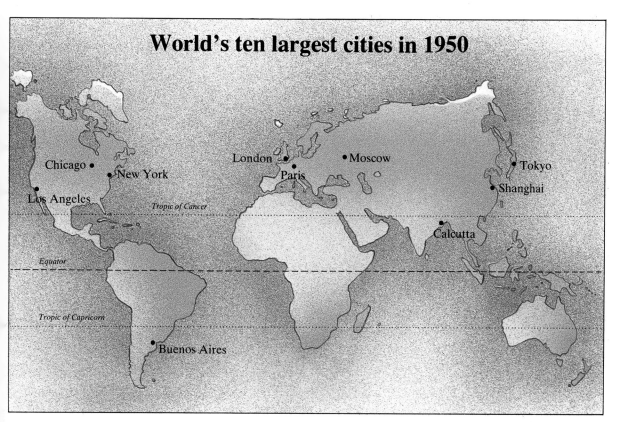

# World's ten largest cities in 1950

- Chicago
- New York
- Los Angeles
- London
- Paris
- Moscow
- Tokyo
- Shanghai
- Calcutta
- Buenos Aires

*Tropic of Cancer*

*Equator*

*Tropic of Capricorn*

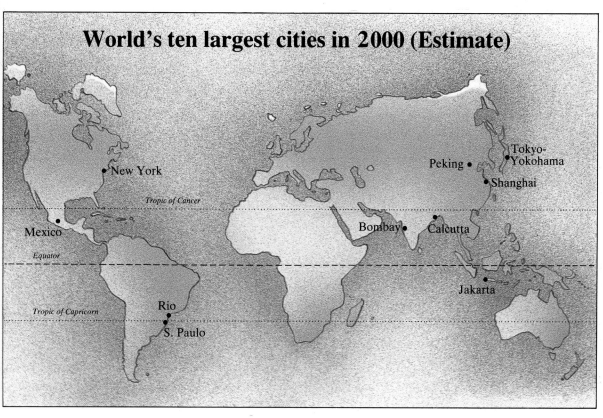

# World's ten largest cities in 2000 (Estimate)

- New York
- Mexico
- Peking
- Tokyo-Yokohama
- Shanghai
- Bombay
- Calcutta
- Jakarta
- Rio
- S. Paulo

*Tropic of Cancer*

*Equator*

*Tropic of Capricorn*

## Concern about nineteenth-century cities

By the nineteenth century, people already felt concern about conditions in the rapidly growing towns and cities. The poor who worked in the new factories lived crowded into bad housing with polluted water supplies and no proper sewers. Charles Dickens, a nineteenth-century British novelist, was horrified by the conditions in some cities. His novel *Hard Times*, published in 1854, contained a vivid description of Coketown, which was probably based on the industrial city of Manchester.

During the course of the nineteenth century, governments gradually began to improve conditions in industrial cities, building sewers and better housing and providing parks and open spaces. Yet even today, the same problems still exist in the world's cities. Mexico City is

*A nineteenth-century drawing of Buffalo, one of the first industrial cities to develop in the eastern United States.*

> It was a town of machinery and tall chimneys, out of which interminable serpents of smoke trailed themselves for ever and ever, and never got uncoiled. It had a black canal in it, and a river that ran purple with ill-smelling dye...
> *Charles Dickens,* Hard Times.

more crowded than nineteenth-century New York, and São Paulo in Brazil is just as noisy and smelly as old Pittsburgh. Must all cities experience pollution and overcrowding, or could these problems be avoided?

# 2
# Keeping the city alive

A city is like a living organism, constantly changing and developing. Some areas of a city may expand and become prosperous, while other areas fall into neglect. Just as all living things need food, water and air, cities also have certain needs, without which they can not function properly.

Certain services are essential to city dwellers. Food and water must be brought into the city from outside, and waste must be taken out of the city and disposed of. Energy supplies are necessary for cooking, heating and industry. A successful city also needs an efficient transportation system, with roads and railroads and sometimes waterways and airports too. These public services make up the economic infrastructure of the city, and without them a city can soon run into difficulties. In an expanding city these public services must be able to keep pace with the new growth.

## Water and sewers

Fresh water is one of the most basic human needs. The well-being of a town or city can perhaps be measured by the adequacy of its water supply. In the developed world, many people take the water supply for granted; everyone has water on tap in their house or apartment, and many people use hundreds of gallons each day. It takes 50 gallons of water to run an automatic washing machine through one cycle, and about 10 gallons to have a bath. In contrast, many people in the developing world have to make do with a dribbling standpipe for their water supply.

Modern industry also uses enormous amounts of water, both for cleaning and as part of manufacturing processes. Without a reliable water supply, industry is crippled.

Keeping water supplies safe and pure is a major problem in some cities. In Calcutta, the water supply system and sewers were built in the last century, when the population of the city was only 600,000. Over ten million people live in the city now, and the old water supply system is unable to cope with the size of the modern

*Not everyone has tapwater in their home. These women in Cape Town, South Africa, have to collect all their water from a communal standpipe in the street.*

*A desalination plant in the Middle Eastern state of Oman.*

population. Some drinking water is drawn straight from the Hooghly River, which runs through Calcutta and which is polluted by the city's untreated sewage.

Waterborne diseases flourish in impure, contaminated water supplies, and outbreaks of serious diseases such as typhoid and cholera are frequent in many tropical and sub-tropical cities. The World Health Organization (WHO) also reports that there is widespread dysentery in 40 percent of cities in the developing world.

Over half the people who live in these cities have no regular, safe water supply.

Competition for fresh water can lead to arguments between different regions and countries. India and Pakistan both accuse one another of taking too much water from the tributaries of the Indus River. The city of Birmingham, England, draws much of its water from central Wales, and some Welsh politicians would like to see a special tax on this valuable export.

Political disagreements can be particularly serious if one country pollutes another's water supply. The Dutch are reliant upon the Rhine River for much of their water. In 1986, the Swiss firm of Sandoz in Basel spilt 100 gallons of diluted atrazin, a powerful weedkiller, into the Rhine. The Dutch authorities, almost 400 miles downstream, were forced to close down one third of their public supplies for several days. There have been at least a dozen other, less serious, incidents where poisonous chemicals have been accidently leaked into the Rhine.

Cities tackle their water supply problems in a variety of different ways. All have been helped by the introduction of cheap plastic water-piping, but building a new water supply system nonetheless remains a costly business. Even today in the old part of central Tokyo, there are no modern sewers, and sewage disposal is still carried out in the old-fashioned way by "night soil men," who empty water closets or pits and carry the sewage away.

Another wealthy city to face water supply problems is Los Angeles. In the 1940s, water was brought from the Colorado River about 400 miles away to supplement local supplies. Today this river water is no longer enough to meet demands, and the city will soon have to build desalination plants along the Pacific Ocean coast. Desalination is the process of taking the salt out of sea water. The ocean is the biggest and most reliable water source for any seaboard city, but desalination is very complicated and expensive, even more costly than piping water over long distances. However, for some cities, desalination may be the only solution to the water shortage.

Hong Kong has a very small surface area over which it can gather rainwater. Traditionally, the city has bought most of its water from neighboring China, but, like Los Angeles, it too is now developing desalination plants.

Another solution to the water shortage is to recycle water. Water can be purified fairly easily, and many cities use the same water more than once. London, for instance, draws much of its water from the Thames River, and Londoners drink water that may have been used three or four times before and purified several times over.

*Women with firewood on the streets of Bombay. In some Indian cities, the poorest people have to forage for firewood.*

## Electricity

Like water, electricity is the lifeblood of all modern cities. The wealthier a city, the more electricity it uses; there is a direct link between people's standard of living and the amount of electricity they use. In Washington D.C., each person uses the power equivalent of 11 tons of coal per year. In Kathmandu, the capital of Nepal, annual power consumption is equivalent to only 22 pounds of coal per person.

Electricity provides heat and light; it is essential to industry; much transportation and many services such as hospitals, radio and television stations and the telephone network depend on it. How many times have you used electricity today and how many electric outlets do you have in your home? How much would your everyday routine be disturbed if there were suddenly no electricity? When the electricity supply failed in New York City on July 13, 1977, there was chaos. No traffic moved, people were trapped in elevators, temperatures in homes and offices dropped and machinery ground to a halt. There was also an increase in crimes of violence and looting.

*In New Zealand, much of the country's electricity is supplied by modern hydroelectric power stations like this one.*

In cities where electricity is not cheaply and easily available to everyone, life is much more difficult. The very poor have to spend long hours foraging or must trek long distances to fetch firewood or dung for heating and cooking. People with enough money must arrange supplies of fuel such as kerosene or bottled gas, which are more expensive and less safe than electricity.

Although most people take their electricity for granted, our current supplies will one day run out. Most electricity is produced from coal, oil or nuclear fuel, all three of which are gradually becoming scarcer. Renewable sources of electricity do exist. The most important of them is hydroelectricity, or water power. However, only a small proportion of the world's electricity is today produced by hydroelectric power stations, and in the future, some cities may be forced to alter radically the way they produce their electricity.

## Transportation

Another vital aspect of city life is an efficient transportation system. Some cities now cover huge areas and are continuing to expand. Greater Chicago measures over 60 miles from north to south. Buenos Aires, the capital of Argentina, is almost 400 miles square in surface area. These huge cities have been made possible only by improved transportation. It allows food and raw materials to be moved easily around the city. It also enables people to move quickly from one part of the city to another, often commuting to and from work, between residential and business and industrial areas. Unless an efficient transportation system is maintained, the city could not function properly.

Methods of transportation vary enormously. In China, a million people commute into central Beijing by bicycle. Many cities have over-ground or underground railroads, trams or buses. In North America, the main means of transportation is usually the car. In some cities in the developing world, people may have to make the journey to work on foot.

The constant ebb and flow of people through the city can create problems of congestion, pollution and accidents. City authorities try to ease these problems in two main ways: by developing the public transportation system or by improving roads to make private transportation easier.

Public transportation is built and run by the city authorities. It usually takes the form of a network of railroads, trams or buses. In some cities, particularly in countries such as West Germany and the Netherlands, there are extremely efficient public transportation systems. By contrast, in many North American cities, the emphasis has been on building freeways and highways. The city of Los Angeles has very little public transportation, and in some districts, up to 30 percent of the land surface is devoted to roads, parking lots and service stations. Which of these two kinds of transportation systems do you think is best?

Private cars have the obvious advantage of being more flexible than even the best public transportation system. With a private car, you can go directly wherever you want, at any time of day. However, cities such as Los Angeles do suffer serious traffic problems. Too many private cars cause appalling traffic jams and delays. Rush-hour traffic in Manhattan moves at only 6 to 7 miles per hour, compared with the average 10 miles per hour traveled by horse-drawn vehicles in the city in 1888! Exhaust fumes are a major source of pollution, and, in addition, car engines add to the already high noise levels in cities.

Perhaps most serious of all is the danger of automobiles. Every day, more people are killed crossing city streets throughout the world than are killed in aircraft accidents during a whole year. Traffic accidents are now one of the main causes of death. How much do we regard them today as unavoidable?

*In many Chinese cities, bicycles are the most common form of transportation.*

The European continent accepts a regular annual massacre of 90,000 citizens on the roads when the same number of deaths in any epidemic would have the whole population screaming for effective counter-measures.

*B. Ward,* The Home of Man.

Building new roads causes problems too. Neighborhoods can be disturbed or even destroyed. In some Middle Eastern cities, the *medinas* or old city centers of narrow winding streets have been laid waste to create wide highways. Paradoxically, building new roads sometimes makes traffic congestion even worse rather than reducing it. The new, bigger roads encourage more people to begin traveling by car, and soon become congested themselves.

A private transportation system also tends to serve the interests of the rich (those who can afford a car) at the expense of poorer people. In the West African cities of Lagos and Accra, recent road development has helped only the small, car-owning élite. Would the money that was needed to build new roads have been better spent on a cheap public transportation system that everyone could use?

*Amsterdam, in the Netherlands, has a modern and efficient public transportation system. The city's trams help reduce pollution levels.*

## Paying for services

No city can survive without the public services discussed in this chapter. It would be hard to live comfortably in a city that had no water, electricity or public transportation. Yet all of these essential services are expensive – who should pay for them?

Some people believe that as many public services as possible should be provided by private companies, and that everyone should pay the same amount for the services they use. Supporters of private enterprise argue that private companies provide better services, though not everyone may be able to afford them.

Other people believe that city authorities should themselves provide essential services. These services should be subsidized by taxes, so that they are cheap and can be used by the whole community.

Which system of paying for public services do you think is best? Do you think your opinion would be different if you were rich or poor?

# 3 Pollution

Pollution is an issue that now attracts more and more news coverage. If you watch a television news program every day for a week, you will almost certainly see at least one item about pollution. Modern cities suffer from a whole range of different types of pollution. Some of this damage to the environment is easily recognizable, but the effects of other forms of pollution, such as noise pollution, are less obvious.

## Chemical pollution

Chemical pollution is perhaps the most common and most widespread type of pollution in the world's cities. It has two main causes: industry and motor-vehicle exhaust fumes.

Pollution from car exhaust fumes is especially bad in some of the most prosperous cities of the developed world. For many people, car ownership is a symbol of wealth; but when hundreds of thousands of cars are concentrated in one small area, the air becomes poisoned by all the exhaust fumes. In recent years, the plight of Tokyo police officers on traffic duty has been highlighted. Wearing face masks, and taking whiffs of oxygen from special containers, they can endure only twenty minutes directing vehicles before removing themselves from the carbon-monoxide fumes.

The air in many of the world's cities is also heavily polluted by industry. Smoke, dust and gases from factories and processing plants can enter the atmosphere and hang in the air for days and weeks on end. In industrial west Chicago, a short walk outside an air-conditioned environment is enough to make your eyes smart. Laundry hanging out to dry is often discolored with flecks of chemicals, and plants and trees are stunted. In Tokyo, much

*Traffic in the Indonesian city of Jakarta. This motorcyclist is wearing a mask to protect himself from the exhaust fumes.*

pollution is caused by the incinerators that burn up the city's rubbish. Japanese tourist brochures say that the country's highest mountain, Mount Fuji, can be seen towering above the capital city; but many people who live in Tokyo will tell you that on most days, Mount Fuji can not be seen for the huge cloud of smoke that hangs over the city like a shroud.

Nor does Tokyo suffer only from air pollution.

In the 1950s and 60s, there were some serious cases of Japanese industry polluting the city's water. Toxic waste, including mercury and cadmium, was poured into the sea and local rivers. Moreover, some factories and companies continued to produce these poisonous materials even after the pollution had been recognized and reported by newspapers and television.

Serious chemical pollution eventually damages the health of all city dwellers. Even if there is no direct health risk from air pollution, no one can avoid being harmed by breathing polluted air every day. However, some people also suffer more immediately from the effects of chemical pollution. Over 41 percent of a U.S. residents live in areas exceeding accept able levels of at least one of these pollutant sulfur dioxide, carbon monoxide, nitroge dioxide, ozone, and lead. These are the onl six pollutants for which the Environmental Pro tection Agency has developed health-based standards; there may be more. In Los Angeles where the nation's smog is thickest, it is no unusual to hear warnings to residents who suf fer from bronchial problems to stay indoors o to use masks if they must go out.

*During the 1950s, London often suffered from thick smog.*

*Women in Bhopal, protesting against the Union Carbide company whose chemical leak caused many deaths and injuries in the city.*

Even more pollution can occur as the result of an industrial accident, particularly in a chemical factory. The worst disaster in recent years was the chemical leak from the Union Carbide factory in the Indian city of Bhopal in 1984. Forty tons of methyl isocyanate leaked from the pesticide factory, and a poisonous gas cloud covered part of the city. Many people died and around 200,000 people suffered injuries to their eyes, throats and lungs.

In recent years, city authorities have become increasingly aware of the need to tackle the problem of pollution. One way of reducing the dangers of pollution is to move industry away from where people live. In developed countries, planners now try to keep people and industry separate, or locate industry right out of the city altogether. However, this kind of planning is often impossible in the rapidly growing cities of the developing world. Governments in poor countries have too little money to spend on planning and can often do nothing to stop the growth of new slums and unofficial shanty towns next to industrial sites.

Although some city authorities have not managed to stop pollution, they try to help people to avoid its worst consequences. In Minneapolis, Minnesota, there are regular announcements on the radio during the rush hour about which freeways are least conjested.

The only completely effective way of preventing industrial pollution is to enforce new laws to restrict the amount of waste that factories can pump into rivers and the atmosphere. Recycling industrial waste is very expensive, and few factories are willing to do it unless forced. However, when it comes to making new anti-pollution laws, governments and city authorities are faced with a dilemma. They may

*Equipment to reduce the amount of pollution caused by a printing works in West Germany. Unfortunately, this kind of equipment is usually expensive, and many firms will not use it unless forced.*

want to restrict and control industry for environmental reasons, but their cities are also dependent upon industry for their prosperity. Factories provide jobs for the city's inhabitants and are a valuable source of taxes. In the modern world, much industry is controlled by multinational corporations. If pollution controls are too strict in one city, it is difficult to stop a multinational corporation from simply moving its actory to another country where there are fewer regulations. City authorities in the developed world are often faced with the hard decision of having to risk either continued pollution or higher unemployment levels. Which of these two problems is worse? Is the pollution of our cities too great a price to pay for high standards of living?

> Improving the environment of the cities is the only way that their economies can be regenerated.
> *Martin Bradshaw, director of the Civic Trust.*

## Noise and alienation

Although chemical pollution is the biggest threat to most modern cities, there are other, more insidious forms of pollution that also make cities unhealthy and unpleasant places in which to live. One aspect of city life that can have harmful effects is noise.

Noise is an inescapable feature of urban life. Cities hum with the sound of traffic, construction sites, trains, police sirens and aircraft overhead. However, in some cities, noise levels are so high as to be actually deafening. Deafness may be caused when people are exposed to more than 87 decibels of sound. Traffic in Rome during the rush hour has recorded over 100 decibels! An average jet plane can register 115 decibels at takeoff, and supersonic aircraft such as Concorde are even louder, reaching over 120 decibels.

High noise levels also contribute to the general stress of city life. The hustle and bustle of long hours of commuting, cramped accommodation and overcrowded streets all combine with noise to make city dwellers feel increasingly stressed. Stress in turn makes people less healthy and more prone to illness, especially high blood pressure and heart disease.

> A great city, a great loneliness.
> *A Latin proverb.*

Another problem is the feeling of loneliness and isolation that some people experience in big cities, particularly if they have. moved to the city from a small town. In small communities people often have much more social contact with their neighbors and colleagues at work. Big cities are more anonymous and it is easy for people living in a city to feel that no one cares about them. Some people have suggested that this sense of alienation is made worse by the unnaturalness of the city surroundings. Store windows are lit by bright, artificial, neon lights, people often travel underground and sometimes must work night shifts instead of more sociable daytime hours. The unnatural environment can increase stress and feelings of alienation.

Cities can be full of excitement and opportunity; but for some people, the stress and loneliness of city life may be the quickest way to an early grave.

*Living in big cities can make people feel lonely and isolated.*

# 4 A home fit to live in

A place to live is one of the most basic human needs, yet many cities provide decent housing for only a small proportion of their inhabitants. In many cities, large numbers of people live in squalid slums or shanty towns. Other people may not have any kind of home at all, but live out on the streets. Why are so few cities able to provide all their inhabitants with a home fit to live in? What are the possible solutions to the housing crisis faced by so many cities?

## Homelessness

There is fierce competition for space in cities. Unlike land in the countryside, urban land is scarce and expensive. Governments and industry can pay high prices for land on which to build factories, offices, roads and public buildings. New housing often comes low down on the list of priorities.

The housing crisis is worst in those cities that are growing most rapidly. As the population increases, competition for housing increases too, and rents spiral upward. The poorest people, usually newcomers to the city, are not able to afford any kind of proper accommodation at all.

The problem of homelessness is often associated with the rapidly expanding cities of the developing world. In Calcutta, India, the work of a Catholic nun, Mother Theresa, has brought the plight of the homeless to people's attention. Mother Theresa founded the Missionaries of Charity in 1950, and the organization now runs over fifty orphanages and hospices for the destitute in India and Bangladesh.

More recently, a film maker, Mira Nair, has drawn people's attention to homelessness in another large Indian city, Bombay. Her film, *Salaam Bombay*, shows the lives of Bombay's homeless street children.

However, homelessness is by no means a problem just in poor countries. In New York, one of the world's richest cities, you can see people sleeping on the sidewalks outside luxury apartment buildings and department stores. "Bag ladies," homeless women who carry all their possessions in one or two plastic bags, are an accepted feature of city life. Some homeless mothers live in New York's subway tunnels, keeping their babies in plastic milk crates instead of cribs. In Washington, D.C., just blocks from the White House and the Capitol Building, old men sleep on heating grates on the sidewalks, trying to keep warm during the winter. All across the country, libraries and other public buildings have become havens for the homeless, who spend their days sleeping at the tables while pretending to read.

In London, England, there are an estimated 30,000 homeless people. Some of these are teenagers who have left home to go to the capital in search of work and a better life. Many can find neither a job nor a place to live and end up out on the streets. It is now common to see homeless young people begging from theater-goers on their way home from a night out in London's West End.

Do you think homelessness can be avoided in big cities? What might be done to reduce it? Do you think that governments have a responsibility to provide everyone with some form of housing? Or is finding a place to live everyone's individual responsibility?

> Governments should demonstrate renewed political commitment to the shelter needs of the poor and disadvantaged by taking significant measures . . . including providing access to land and ensuring security of tenure in squatter settlements, adapting codes and regulations to the needs of the people.
> *Resolution 41/190 of the United Nations Assembly.*

**Right** *A slum in the Indian city of Pune.*

## Slums and shanty towns.

In addition to the homeless, millions of city dwellers live in substandard or inadequate housing. In some cities, the housing shortage forces the poorest people into slums, in the old, overcrowded buildings that have been abandoned by wealthier city dwellers. In the developing world, the only way for the poor and homeless to find shelter may be by building themselves shacks, using old wood, cardboard, corrugated iron, cloth, palm leaves or anything else that they can find. Shanty towns spring up on any empty waste land, and even on roadsides and railroad embankments. In Cairo in Egypt and Lima in Peru, rubbish dumps are a favorite site for shanty towns. Here, even children can help to earn their keep by searching through the waste for anything they can retrieve and sell.

*A homeless teenager in London. Who should be responsible for finding him somewhere to live?*

In some cities, shanty towns are now huge; and in Calcutta, for instance, there is so little room in the slums that there are even landlords who rent out *bustees*, primitive tents, to those people who can afford them.

Conditions in the shanty towns are squalid and unhealthy. Because the shanties are unofficial, and usually illegal, they are ignored by city authorities, and receive none of the services taken for granted in other parts of the city. Electricity is rare. There are no sewers or proper water supplies, and diseases such as cholera and dysentery are often widespread. There are other dangers in the shanty towns too. In Rio de Janeiro in Brazil, the *favellas* are built on steep slopes and enjoy spectacular

24

**Above** *Council housing in southern England. A way of reducing the housing shortage is for local councils to build rented accommodation.*

**Right** *A favella, or shanty town, in Brazil. Shanties built on slopes like this are in constant danger from landslides.*

views over the glorious Copocobana beaches; but after heavy rain whole shanty towns can be swept away by landslides. In some countries, people also live in fear that their shanties may be bulldozed by the government. During the late 1970s, the Indian government of Mrs. Gandhi, embarrassed by the shanties around Delhi, knocked many of them down without providing new housing for any of the people who lived in them. The poverty of a shanty town might shock a North American or European visitor, but a shanty is the only home that many people have, and is far better than no home at all.

*Modern suburban sprawl in Virginia.*

### Suburbs and inner cities

The most common way of providing good, new housing is for cities to develop suburbs or satellite towns. In New York, the high cost of living and increasing crime in the city center, Manhattan, have been the main causes of decentralization. Although it is still fashionable to live in Manhattan, some companies, such as Pepsi Cola, have moved outside the city to new suburban sites, taking their workers with them.

The extra space in the suburbs means that houses can be larger, with yards, and there is more room for recreational activities. However, suburbs can cause problems too. Suburban sprawl can use up valuable agricultural land. It also increases the surface area of the city enormously. People then have to spend longer commuting to work, and it becomes harder to move from one part of the city to another. Some cities, such as Bombay which is built on the end of a peninsula, face particular problems. Because Bombay is almost surrounded by the sea, it has been forced to grow northwards along the peninsula, and the outermost suburbs are now located far from the center.

The growth of suburbs also alters the status of the inner city. As the wealthier and more powerful city dwellers move out to the suburbs, the inner city may be left neglected. In recent decades, inner-city decay has affected many cities in North America and Europe. City authorities concentrate on providing services to the new suburbs, and the poorer people who are left in the inner city do not themselves have the money to repair the old buildings. Some inner cities have quite literally begun to decay, and crumbling buildings and pot-holed roads have become a common sight. At the very worst, the inner city can become a slum, such as Harlem in New York, where many of the city's poorest inhabitants live crowded in old tenement buildings.

When businesses move out of large cities, they often take hundreds and even thousands of jobs away with them. Manufacturing plants in big cities must pay high taxes and high wages. In smaller towns, especially those with high unemployment, people are willing to do the same work for less money because their cost of living is lower.

Governments have now recognized the problem of inner cities, and in some countries measures have been taken to improve conditions there. In Boston and Baltimore, impressive new offices, hotels, conference centers and shopping malls have revitalized the city centers. In other cities, such as Philadelphia and New Orleans, there is also a natural trend for wealthier people to move back into the inner cities from the suburbs. Perhaps because of time wasted in commuting to and from work, and the more exciting cultural and artistic life

*Financial neglect has caused the decay of inner-city districts such as Harlem in New York.*

of the inner cities, more people are buying homes in the older parts of these cities. Many older houses are being restored by private owners. This type of renovation is often referred to as gentrification.

The process of gentrification can revitalize communities and stop inner-city decay, but it also raises house prices and rents, so that poorer people are driven out of certain areas.

*A garden center and new housing in inner London. In recent years there has been a trend toward inner-city renewal, funded by both government grants and private investment.*

Even in the prosperous, gentrified districts of London and New York, there is still the problem of providing cheap accommodation that everyone can afford.

28

# 5
# Divisions in the city

The world's cities are melting pots; a wide variety of people from many different cultures and backgrounds live side by side in them. Rich and poor, black and white, Jew and Muslim, all find themselves living in the same community. In cities, the divisions between people seem much more obvious and immediate; and sometimes these differences can lead to bitter and even violent conflicts.

## Rich and poor

> A city, however small, is divided into two, the city of the poor and the city of the rich; they are at war with one another.
> *Plato,* The Republic.

Most cities are centers of wealth. Their prosperity comes from being important seats of government, or centers of industry and trade. Yet many cities also contain huge concentrations of poor people. What causes this division between rich and poor, and what, if anything, can be done to reduce it?

The reasons for poverty vary from city to city, but there are certain causes that are common to most cities. In many cities wealth and poverty seem to go hand in hand, as the wealth of the city attracts poor people from outside. Particularly in developing countries, where there is rapid urban growth, the poor from the countryside may go to the city in the hope of finding work. However, conditions in the city are usually far from ideal.

Few immigrants in the city are able to do skilled work, and most find themselves left with the dull, badly paid jobs that no one else wants.

Many have to take jobs in factories, become servants, or work as unskilled laborers, often in temporary employment in the building industry. Others are unable to find any kind of paid work and are forced to earn a living by doing odd jobs, perhaps by selling newspapers or washing cars. Even if they earn more money in the city than in the countryside, people are not necessarily better off, since food and rent may be much more expensive in the city.

Industry does not necessarily help the poor either. If there is an industrial recession, factory workers are the first people to be laid off; and

*A Muslim (left) and Orthodox Jews (right) in Jerusalem. There is often conflict between the two religious groups in the city.*

*Selling small items of food or drink is another way of earning a little money. Many street vendors have no home and sleep out in the open at night.*

even during periods of prosperity, factory workers in developing countries may remain poor. Employers can keep wage rates low because they know that a new wave of immigrants will be prepared to work at any price and replace those workers who protest or have gone on strike.

In some countries industrialization has certainly increased everyone's standard of living. South Korea, for instance, has undergone an economic miracle over the past twenty years, and from being a very poor country, it has become one of the world's biggest industrial nations with high standards of living. Yet in other parts of the world, such as India, new industry has made only a few people more wealthy, while the majority of factory workers remain as poor as ever. Can you think of any reasons for this difference?

If the problem of poverty is not tackled, tension between rich and poor in the city quickly increases. In cities where large numbers of poor people are gathered together in one place, discontent can easily become revolt; many revolutions have been triggered by a sudden increase in food prices or unemployment which affects the poor most. Even if it does not lead to organized revolution, resentment against the wealthy can result in spontaneous rioting; during 1981, there was serious rioting in the poorest areas of the British cities of Bristol and Liverpool.

Governments can respond to this kind of rioting in two ways; they may try to reduce the poverty that causes discontent, but they may also react by introducing repressive measures to control the poor. As many as two thousand years ago, the rulers of ancient Rome knew about the importance of controlling the poor with a policy of "bread and circuses."

*A boy working on a building site in Cairo, Egypt. Many poor people must take badly paid jobs as unskilled laborers if they move to a rapidly growing city.*

Poverty can also lead directly to crime, particularly if a city has no welfare system. Unemployment and destitution then drive many people to petty crime, such as pickpocketing, shop lifting and handbag snatching, just to survive. This petty crime may later become more serious, as people turn to mugging or drug peddling to make a living. However, crimes are committed by the rich too, and the poorest cities of the world do not always have the worst crime records. Calcutta, for instance, seems to have less crime than Detroit, Washington or Houston, all of which have been described as the "murder capitals" of the United States. By American standards Detroit does have much poor quality housing, unemployment and low educational standards, yet most of the population is wealthy in comparison with Calcutta. Can you think of any reasons to explain this difference in levels of crime?

*A woman begging in India (left) and an old man begging on the streets of New York (right). Poverty is a problem in cities in both the developing and the developed world.*

## Race and religion

The conflict between rich and poor is only one of many divisions affecting the world's cities. Often a group of people may be divided from the rest of the city not only because they are poor but for another reason too, such as their race or religion.

Some cities contain ghettos, run-down districts of the city in which people of one particular culture or background all live together, separate from the rest of the city. The people in the ghetto may stand out from the rest of the community because of their race or skin color,

*Rioting in the London district of Brixton, 1981. Brixton is one of the city's poorest areas.*

such as in the Bedford-Stuyvesant area of Brooklyn, which has become a black ghetto; or they may be different because of their religion, as in the Jewish ghettos in some of the world's cities. However, many cities have areas where one particular racial group has settled, but which are not described as ghettos. There are Chinatowns, for instance, in San Francisco, London and the Australian city of Brisbane, but the people who live there share in the general prosperity of the city and are not especially underprivileged. Ghettos exist where the inhabitants are not properly integrated within the city and are discriminated against by the rest of the community. Not surprisingly, people who live in ghettos feel a strong sense of resentment against the rest of the city, and their anger can spill over into violence.

Probably the worst examples of ghettos and racial discrimination in the world occur in South Africa. There, the white government, with its system of apartheid, forces black and colored people to live separated from whites in special city areas called townships. One of the biggest townships is that of Soweto (the South West Township) about 12 miles outside of Johannesburg. More than a million people live in the small, crowded homes of Soweto; most of them must make the long journey into Johannesburg to work every day, using special trains and buses. This township is one of the centers of black protest against apartheid, but it is often also the scene of harsh government repression.

*A street in Chinatown, New York.*

Some of the world's cities are split not by racial but by religious divisions. In Northern Ireland, Belfast is divided between the Protestant and Catholic communities. Catholics make up 31 percent of the population, Protestants 59 percent. On the whole, Catholics are poorer than Protestants and many feel that they have been discriminated against. Some Catholics would like Northern Ireland to become part of the Irish Republic to the south, while Protestants wish to remain part of the United Kingdom. In Belfast, Protestants and Catholics go to different schools, attend different clubs and, above all, live in different areas of the city. Since 1969, there has been constant violence in Belfast between members of the two communities, and hundreds of people have been killed over the years.

Beirut, the capital of the Lebanon, has also seen dreadful conflict between its different religious communities. For many years, various Muslim and Christian groups lived together peacefully, but internal problems and foreign pressure caused a civil war to break out, and Beirut is now split into opposing districts.

Do you think it is inevitable that different racial and religious groups have violent conflicts? Can you think of any ways of helping different communities to live together peacefully in the world's cities?

**Above** *The black township of Soweto, outside Johannesburg in South Africa.*

**Below** *The system of apartheid has meant that black and white South Africans even have to use separate beaches.*

# 6
# Who controls the city?

Organizing the daily life of a city is a complicated matter. Streets must be kept clean, schoolteachers paid, hospitals built, water supplies checked and law and order maintained. Every city needs officials to arrange these essential services.

In small cities, administration is not too difficult. It is possible for administrators to know all the districts of the city and all the workers in a particular department. A housing officer, for instance, can know all the streets, the different communities and their special problems.

However, it is much harder to administrate today's larger cities. In a city with six or seven million inhabitants, it is impossible for an official to understand all the problems, or even all the aspects of any one problem. Few people are able to gain an overview of what is happening in the city. Officials are often unable to respond quickly to its changing needs.

Most large cities now have so many administrative departments that any decision takes a long time. In order to talk to one another, officials must arrange meetings weeks in advance. Officials spend an enormous amount of time and energy just in communicating with each other, and even then, different departments may not be able to agree on the best way of tackling a problem. To fill a hole in the road may take an inspector, surveyor, estimator, clerical officer, road worker and checker!

*Refuse collectors in Bangkok. Organizing services like refuse collection is a vital aspect of governing a city.*

As a bureaucracy grows, opportunities for corruption increase too. Officials might be tempted to accept bribes, or even to embezzle city funds. Almost every city in the world has at least one notorious case of corruption. In 1989, the U.S. Department of Housing and Urban Development (HUD) was accused of mismanaging funds that were supposed to go into programs to provide better and more affordable housing in the nation's cities.

Do you think there is any way that this kind of corruption can be avoided?

## Power in the city

As we saw in the previous chapter, people who live in cities are often divided into opposing groups. Each group struggles to increase its power and control within the city government.

The city of Chicago was controlled by one group of citizens for some thirty years. Led by Mayor Richard Daley, Catholics of Irish descent dominated the city's government and administration from 1955 to 1975. All civil servants in Chicago, from the chief of police to the bus drivers, had to be appointed with the mayor's approval. Daley made sure that all the important jobs were given to Democrats and

*Richard Daley, mayor of Chicago from 1955 to 1975.*

Irish Catholics. The corruption and nepotism of Daley's administration was well known; yet it was largely ignored, because many people felt that "Daley's boys" kept the city functioning well, and Daley was re-elected with a large majority for twenty years.

Other U.S. cities are governed in a completely different way from Daley's Chicago. In Los Angeles, the structure of government means that power is split among many different people and authorities. The city covers a huge area and it is more than 70 miles wide. It contains over two hundred separate communities and more than seventy independent city units. Each unit has a separate council and facilities, and its own ideas about how to get things done. The advantage of the Los Angeles system of government is that it gives many different people the chance to exercise some power. However, the city also faces problems. It is difficult for all the different groups to agree on one single plan for development, and a coordinated attack on some of the city's civic problems is almost impossible. Sometimes, it can seem as if no one is in control in Los Angeles.

Power struggles are not confined just to groups within the city. Sometimes the conflict is at the higher level of the state or national government versus the city.

New York City has a long-standing dispute with the New York state government in the state capital, Albany. The state government decides how much money should be spent on providing public services in New York. Because the state wants to keep taxes low, it gives the mayor of New York too little money to carry out all of his policies. In the mid 1970s, the city came close to bankruptcy. It was forced to dismiss teachers and members of the police force, and was only rescued by a short-term, federal-government loan.

The United States has a complicated system of funding city services and projects. Cities rely on both state and federal funds. Whenever federal funds are granted, they are accompanied by certain regulations. Schools and libraries that receive federal funds, for instance, must agree not to discriminate on the basis of race, creed, national or ethnic origin, age, marital status, sex, or handicap when they hire employees and when they decide who will attend the school or use the library.

Cities throughout the world have disagreements with their national governments. In Canada, Montreal and Toronto can be restricted by the capital, Ottawa. In Australia, the authorities in the old, established cities of Sydney and Melbourne do not always agree with the national government in the modern capital city of Canberra.

In the city states of ancient Greece, it was possible for power to be shared democratically among the citizens. Whenever an important decision had to be made, all the citizens gathered together in a large crowd (or *demos*) to discuss the issue until they reached an agreement. How much is it possible for every citizen to have a voice in today's big cities? Does power have to be given to just a few people, and if it does, who should be allowed to govern our cities, and how?

**Below** *County Hall, the headquarters of the Greater London Council. Despite strong protests, the city council was abolished by central government in 1986.*

**Right** *Although New York is one of the largest and most important cities in the developed world, the amount of money to be spent on city services is decided by the state government.*

# 7 Planning for the future

This book has discussed many of the problems that affect today's cities. How far can we hope to solve these problems by careful planning for the future?

As early as the nineteenth century, some people were arguing that cities should be better planned. The French writer Alexis de Tocqueville visited Manchester in the 1840s

*The model town of Saltaire, in West Yorkshire, England. Saltaire was one of the first, nineteenth-century experiments in town planning. It was built by the mill owner Sir Titus Salt to house the workers from his factory.*

and was as disturbed as Charles Dickens was by the conditions that he found there. De Tocqueville believed that much of the squalor was caused by the lack of proper planning.

> Everything in the exterior appearance of the city attests the individual powers of man; nothing the directing power of society. At every turn human liberty shows its capricious creative force. There is no trace of the slow continuous action of government.
> *A. de Tocqueville*, Journeys to England and Ireland.

However, even during the early nineteenth century, some people were already experimenting with town planning. A number of rich industrialists used their money to build new, "model" towns for their workers. One of the earliest and most famous of these was New Lanark, built in Scotland by the factory owner Robert Owen in 1816.

*Government buildings in the specially planned Brazilian capital of Brasilia.*

Since New Lanark, many other new towns and cities have been specially planned in different parts of the world. In Brazil, the city of Brasilia was founded on a carefully chosen site in 1956 to be the city's new federal capital. Another specially built capital city is Canberra in Australia; the city was planned to be as spacious as possible, and covers a ground area larger than London although it has only about one fiftieth of London's population. In northern India, the new city of Chandigarh has a similar spacious layout, planned by the Swiss architect, Le Corbusier.

## What makes for good planning?

Although by building a brand new city many urban problems can be avoided, most planners are occupied in trying to solve the problems of existing cities. Some of the ideas that have been put forward for improving cities can seem bizarre. One architect, for instance, has suggested building a marina city floating on a huge concrete raft in the North Sea off the British coast. Hundreds of apartments would be built to face south, and the raft itself would be programmed to turn slowly during the day, following the course of the sun!

However, ideas that seem weird to us today may be practical sometime in the future. Only thirty years ago, the idea of pedestrian malls was new and unusual, but nowadays almost every city in the developed world has one. Some cities have even developed the idea of pedestrian malls one stage further. Montreal in Canada has subways, with layers of stores beneath the streets linked to underground railroad entrances. In Minnesota, St. Paul and Minneapolis have an even more unusual "skyway," a system of covered walkways where people can cross from building to building at second-floor level above the street. During the harsh, Midwestern winter, people can keep dry and warm as they move from store to store; street congestion is reduced, and there are small shops, such as travel agencies and shoeshine booths, on the walkways themselves.

Pedestrian malls have proved to be a popular planning idea, but other types of developments have been less successful. Sometimes planners have been accused of not understanding the needs of ordinary people, and may even have made conditions in cities worse rather than better. In the 1960s, much of the old, terraced housing in British cities such as Manchester and Liverpool was pulled down, and people were moved into new high-rise apartments. Whole neighborhoods were destroyed, and many people felt that the new housing was unfriendly and impersonal. Some people in Liverpool say that town planners have done more damage to the city than the German bombing during World War II.

*The Australian capital of Canberra was founded in 1911 on a carefully chosen site. It contains the Australian parliament and many government buildings.*

In the developing world too, planners have sometimes lost sight of the real needs of the community. One problem is that planners and governments may have tried to imitate cities in the developed world, without taking all the different conditions into account. Ibadan, in Nigeria, for instance, had an old-fashioned, but busy, public slaughter yard. The government decided to replace it with a modern, Western-style slaughter house called an abattoir. Although the new abattoir was clean and efficient, it was too expensive for many market people to use. The price of meat went up, and many cattle drovers soon became unemployed.

It is also important for planners to think of the needs of the whole community and not just the interests of a small and powerful élite. Governments may be tempted to spend money on projects that increase the prestige of the ruling class but do not benefit the majority of the people. The Indian government was criticized in the early 1980s for building a new sports complex to house the Asian Games in Delhi. The sports stadiums and athletes' village were admired by millions of television spectators; but could the money have been better spent in different ways?

*Tower blocks like these were a popular solution to housing shortages in the 1960s.*

New plans often lead to arguments between groups of people, some of whom may support the new development and others who oppose it. Planners talk about the NIMBY (Not In My Back Yard) syndrome, when new developments are opposed by groups of people who are concerned only about the local effects of plans rather than their wider importance. Who should have the power to make the final planning decisions about city development?

The most important planning decisions of all concern the size of the world's cities. By the year 2000, cities such as Mexico City and São Paulo will have over twenty million inhabitants. Governments must surely begin to ask themselves whether these cities are not simply too large to function properly. What is the optimum size for a city?

No city should be too large for a man to walk out of in a morning.
*C.Connolly,* The Unquiet Grave.

In some countries, governments have already begun to restrict the growth of cities. In Britain, an Act of Parliament in 1947 created a "green belt" around London, in which no new buildings are allowed. The trend toward smaller cities could also be encouraged by technological changes. As communications improve, there may be less need for people to live in cities at all. Within the next few decades, more people in the developed world may begin to work from home, using computer terminals that are connected to a main computer many miles away.

As the world's cities continue to grow, the difficulties that they face will not go away without human intervention. Congestion, pollution, and homelessness will remain features of city life for many years to come. Yet there is no need for our cities to be squalid and unpleasant.

The bustle and vitality of city life is exciting, and in spite of all their problems, many cities can still be enriching places in which to live. The human race has the scientific and technological knowledge to control its environment. The urban crisis poses a challenge – will we meet it with determination and build cities of which we can be proud? Or will cities continue to contain all the worst aspects of modern-day life?

**Right** *The Albert Dock in the British port of Liverpool. Buildings in this depressed inner-city area have been restored with the help of government funds.*

**Below** *Crowds in the Indian city of Madras. Cities in the developing world are now growing faster and larger than ever before.*

# Glossary

**Artisan**   A skilled worker who makes things.

**Apartheid**   A political system that separates people of different races and ethnic groups and forces them to live in different areas.

**Congestion**   Overcrowding.

**Decentralization**   The policy of persuading people to move out of crowded cities to other areas.

**Desalination plant**   A factory that removes the salt from sea water to make drinking water.

**Destitute**   Without money or any means of looking after oneself.

**Developing world**   The poorest countries of the world, which are trying to develop modern industries. Developing countries are sometimes called the "Third World."

**Developed world**   The richest and economically most powerful countries in the world. Sometimes called the "First World."

**Economic infrastructure**   Services such as roads, railroads and telephones that are needed in an industrial society.

**Élite**   The group of people with the most money, power and other advantages.

**Gentrification**   The process of renovating old houses so that they have better facilities, but also become more expensive.

**Hydroelectricity**   Electricity produced by water power.

**Industrialization**   The development of modern industries so that a country's economy is based upon industry and not agriculture.

**Industrial Revolution**   The period in history, from the late eighteenth century onward, when European countries began to develop machinery and factories.

**Integration**   Joining together to make a united whole. Cultural integration is the process by which different groups of people live peacefully together in one community.

**Multinational corporation**   A large company that has branches in many different countries.

**Nepotism**   The favoring of a relation or friend by giving them a job or promotion.

**Organism**   A living thing.

**Paradox**   Someone or something that seems to show contradictions.

**Prestige**   High reputation or standing.

**Private enterprise**   An economic undertaking (such as building a new factory) that does not receive any support from the government.

**Public services**   Services that are supplied by the government, sometimes supported by money from taxes.

**Racial discrimination**   Treating someone differently because of his or her nationality or skin color.

**Shanty town**   A town of makeshift houses, built from scrap materials on waste land.

**Socialist**   Someone who believes that industry and wealth should be owned by the community as a whole.

**Social structure**   The way in which society is made up of different groups.

**Subsidize**   To give financial support to something or someone.

**Surplus**   An amount that is more than what is needed or used.

**Toxic**   Poisonous.

**Township**   In South Africa, a township is a suburb where black or colored people are forced to live, separated from whites.

**Urbanization**   The development of towns and cities, resulting in a higher proportion of the population living in urban areas.

# Books to read

*Cities Under Stress* by Kathlyn Gay
        (Watts, 1985)
*The Growth of Cities* by Trudy Hanmer
        (Watts, 1985)
*How the World's First Cities Began* by
        Arthur S. Gregor (Dutton, 1967)
*The City: Yesterday, Today, and Tomorrow*
        by Emrys Jones and Eleanor Van Zandt
        (Doubleday, 1974)
*Cities 2000* by Robert Royston (Facts on File,
        1985)

# Further information

If you wish to find out more about some of the issues discussed in this book, you might find the following addresses useful:

National Clean Air Coalition
801 Pennsylvania Avenue SE, 3rd Fl.
Washington, D.C. 20003
Conducts workshops for the public on clean air issues.

National Urban Coalition
1120 G St., NW, Suite 900
Washington, D.C. 20005
Seeks to improve the quality of life and opportunities for the disadvantaged in urban areas.

Experimental Cities, Inc.
PO Box 731
Pacific Palisades, CA 90272
Looks for innovative solutions to urban deterioration.

ACCION International
1385 Cambridge St.
Cambridge, MA 02139
Specializes in assistance to local organizations reaching small enterprises in urban and rural areas in the Americas.

First published in the
United States in 1990 by
Rourke Enterprises, Inc.
Vero Beach, FL 32964

Printed in Italy

# Index

# Picture Acknowledgments

Bradford Tourist Office 40; Chapel Studios 13, 15, 30, 32 (left), 36; Mary Evans Picture Library 10; Format Photographers 19 (Sue Darlow), 33 (Joanne O'Brien); Hutchinson Picture Library 6, 24 (below), 28 (Christine Pemberton), 29 (Melanie Friend), 38, 42 (Bernard Régent); LINK/Orde Eliason 11, 24, 29 (above and below), 35; LINK/Kim Naylor 44; Christine Osborne *cover*, Topham Picture Library 18, 32 (right), 37, 43; Wayland Picture Library 14, 45; ZEFA *frontispiece*, 7, 12, 16, 17, 20, 21, 23, 25 (above), 26, 27, 31, 34, 39, 41. Maps are by Stephen Wheele.

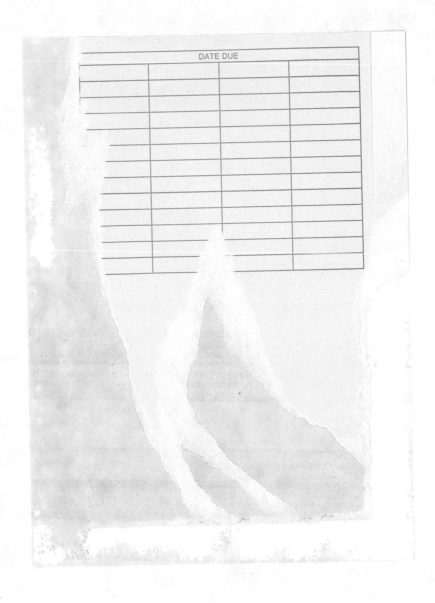

DATE DUE